Children's Atlas
of
Animals

Contents

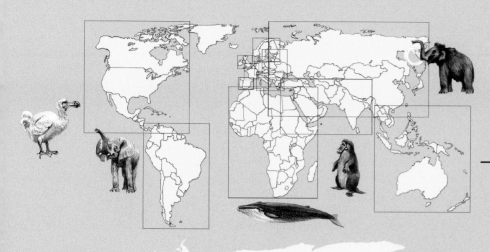

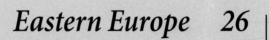

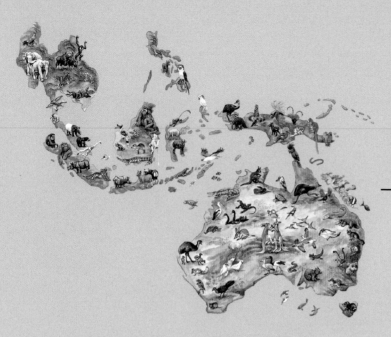

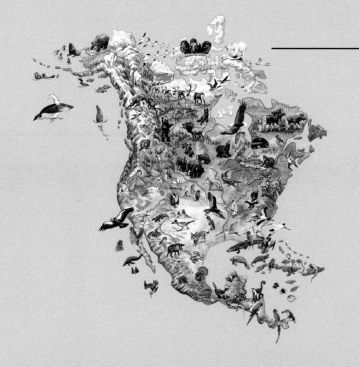

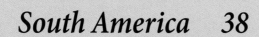

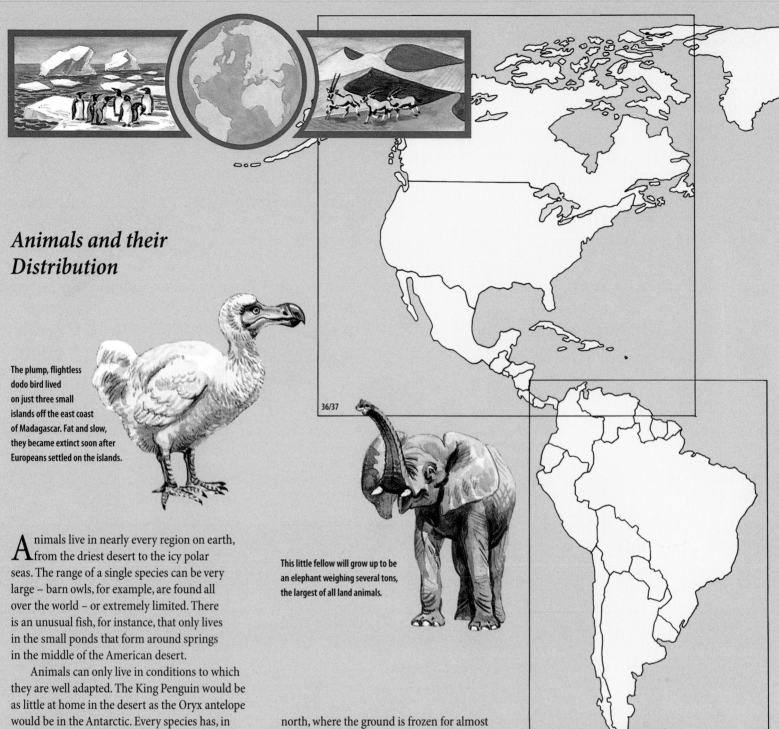

Animals and their Distribution

The plump, flightless dodo bird lived on just three small islands off the east coast of Madagascar. Fat and slow, they became extinct soon after Europeans settled on the islands.

This little fellow will grow up to be an elephant weighing several tons, the largest of all land animals.

A nimals live in nearly every region on earth, from the driest desert to the icy polar seas. The range of a single species can be very large – barn owls, for example, are found all over the world – or extremely limited. There is an unusual fish, for instance, that only lives in the small ponds that form around springs in the middle of the American desert.

Animals can only live in conditions to which they are well adapted. The King Penguin would be as little at home in the desert as the Oryx antelope would be in the Antarctic. Every species has, in the course of its existence, evolved to survive in a very specific environment. Perhaps it has an especially thick fur coat, or the ability to live for an extended period of time without water. Animal habitats are defined by climate and the kind of plant life that grows there. Location also matters. Does the habitat lie on the equator, or in a snow-covered polar region? The landscape features, like mountains and lakes, also play a part, as does the distance from the sea. Forests only grow where the great trees can draw sufficient nutrients from a soil deep enough to accommodate their roots, preferably in a region where there is enough water all year round. Forest zones include the taiga, with its fir trees and birches, the temperate forest zone, where the trees are deciduous, mountain forests and, of course, the tropical rainforest. The steppes in northern Eurasia, prairies in North America and savannahs in the tropical south are examples of open grasslands, an environment where forests cannot gain a foothold. Far to the

north, where the ground is frozen for almost the entire year, mosses, grasses and lichens are characteristic of the Arctic tundra. Deserts are regions where very little rain falls and life is difficult for even the smallest plants and animals.

But it is not the environment alone that determines an animal's distribution on earth. Obstacles like seas, mountain ranges and deserts can stop a species from spreading further. As a result, each continent is home to

its own unique range of animals. Zoologists divide the earth geographically into six faunal zones: the High Arctic, Neo-tropical, Ethiopian, Oriental, Australasian and Oceanic.

Often, the present-day distribution of an animal species also provides information about the history of the earth itself. We know, for example, that 270 million years ago there was just one giant continent, Pangaea. Over time, and very slowly, perhaps just 4 in (10 cm) per year, the continents we know today drifted apart, to be separated by the great seas and oceans.

During the ice ages, the dropping sea level left land bridges between many of the continents for an extended period of time. North America and Asia, for example, were joined near Alaska.

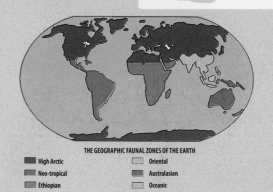

THE GEOGRAPHIC FAUNAL ZONES OF THE EARTH

- High Arctic
- Neo-tropical
- Ethiopian
- Oriental
- Australasian
- Oceanic

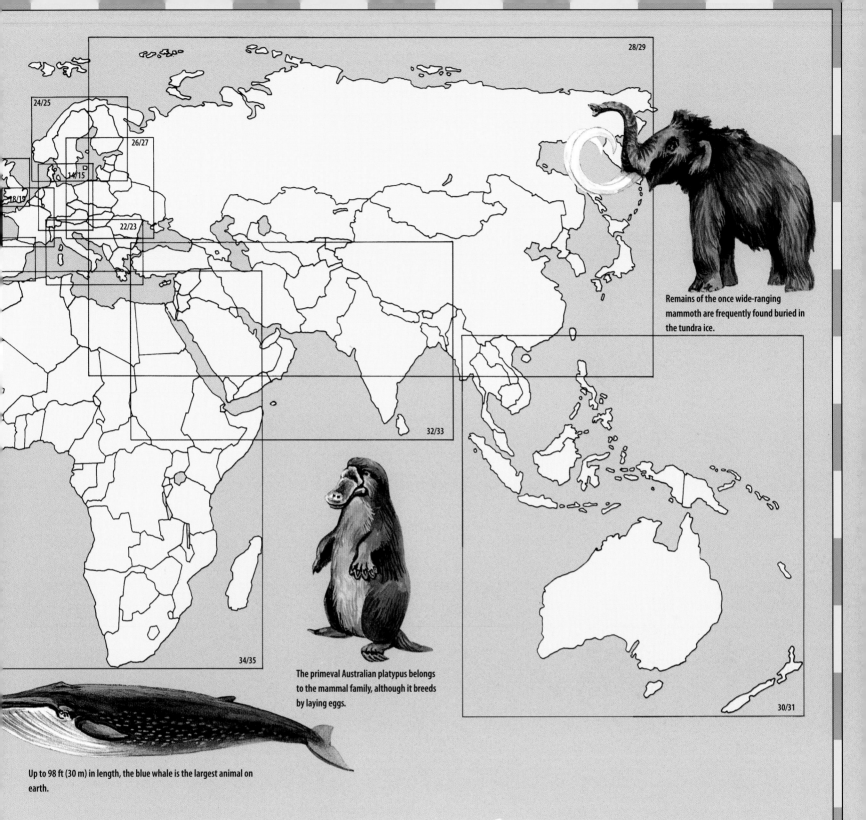

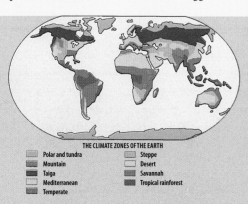

Remains of the once wide-ranging mammoth are frequently found buried in the tundra ice.

The primeval Australian platypus belongs to the mammal family, although it breeds by laying eggs.

Up to 98 ft (30 m) in length, the blue whale is the largest animal on earth.

The land bridge of Central America is still present today. The oddest animal worlds are the ones with many so-called "primeval" (early) species, like Australia. Their existence suggests a long period of isolation. In contrast, finding the same, or closely related, animal species on different continents indicates that there was once a physical connection between the land masses. Nevertheless, some animals manage to migrate to far distant lands despite geographical obstacles. Flying animals such as bats and birds have little difficulty crossing mountains and seas. Insects can travel long distances on the wind. Even land animals have succeeded in settling distant islands, travelling on floating tree trunks or rafts of vegetation. In this way lemurs came to Madagascar and the giant land tortoise made it to the Galapagos Islands. Finally, humans have also played a role in assisting the movement of animals between continents. Mice, rabbits and feral domestic animals can arrive in a different habitat via ship or airplane. People also tend to take along animals they find useful when they migrate. This is how the horse came from Europe to North America, and how forest animals suitable for hunting arrived in England from Asia.

THE CLIMATE ZONES OF THE EARTH

Polar and tundra
Mountain
Taiga
Mediterranean
Temperate
Steppe
Desert
Savannah
Tropical rainforest

270 million years ago, there was just one giant continent, called Pangaea.

Germany, Austria and Switzerland

Dense beech and oak forest once covered most of Germany, Switzerland and Austria. Today, a great many people live in this part of Europe, and the primeval forest has long been cleared. The trees growing today are non-native species grown for their timber. There is very little untouched, natural forest left. Small stretches can be found in the Bavarian Forest, Harz Mountains and Pfalz Forest. Happily, red deer, wildcats, wild pigs and the mufflon, a kind of sheep, are equally at home in a forest planted by humans as they are on their native mountain slopes. There are also many animals adapted to the drier steppe environment now living in the treeless landscape of field, meadow and hedgerow. The long-legged hare, as well as numerous species of butterfly and grasshopper, are among the species that enjoy farm life. The common buzzard, expanding its territory ever further westward, finds agricultural areas ideal for the hunt.

The great bustard, common in the eastern steppe regions, has recently been sighted in Germany. From a distance, this shy, heavy

The bearded vulture died out in the Alpine regions during the last century. Today, efforts are being made to

BALTIC SEA

NORTH SEA

0   100   200 km

1 Mole
2 Wild rabbit
3 Hare
4 Mountain (snow) hare
5 Alpine marmot
6 Beaver
7 Edible dormouse
8 White mouse
9 Fox
10 Tree martin
11 Mouse weasel
12 European otter
13 Wild cats
14 Seal
15 Wild pig
16 Red deer
17 Fallow deer
18 Roe deer
19 Ibex
20 Mufflon sheep
21 Chamois
22 Great crested grebe
23 Great white stork
24 Black stork
25 Sea eagle
26 Golden eagle
27 Goshawk
28 Common buzzard
29 Osprey
30 Peregrine falcon
31 Capercaillie (grouse)
32 Black grouse
33 Hazel grouse
34 Partridge
35 Great bustard
36 Crane
37 Oyster catcher
38 Lapwing
39 Ringed plover
40 Black-tailed godwit
41 Sandpiper
42 Redshank
43 Dunlin
44 Common snipe
45 Ibis
46 Little owl
47 Eagle owl
48 Alpine swift

14

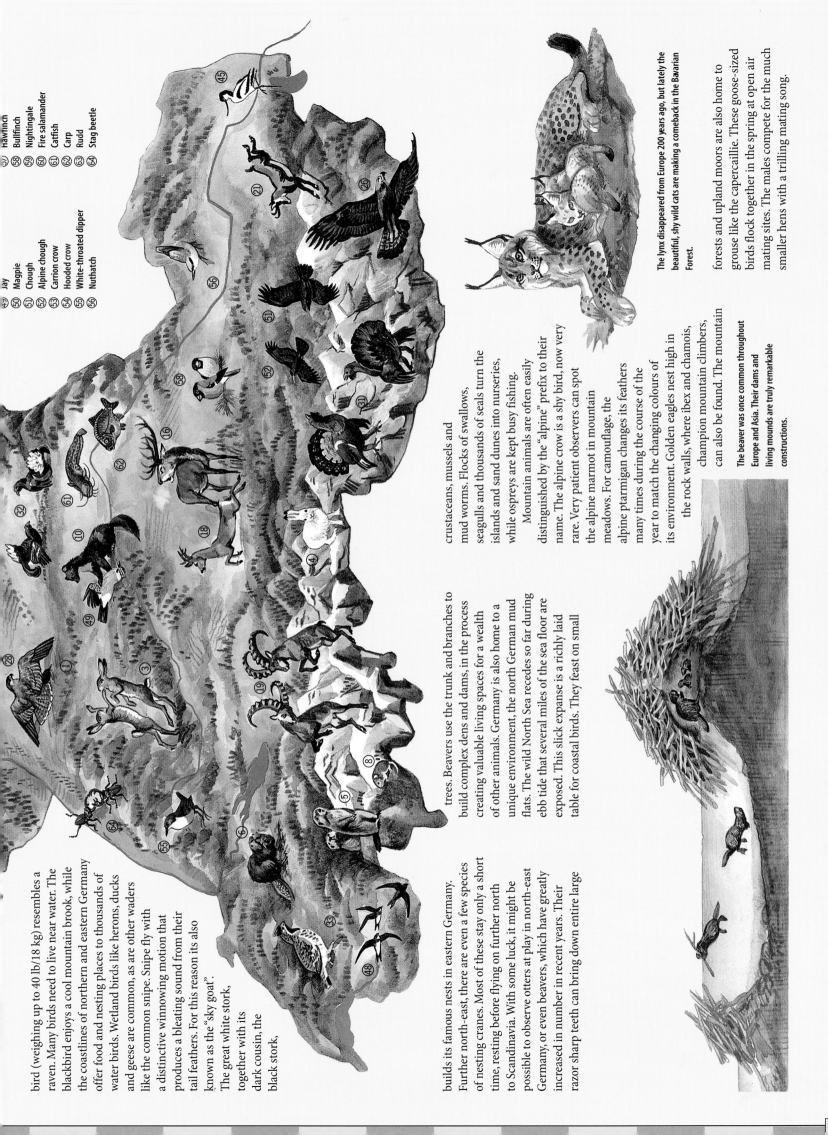

bird (weighing up to 40 lb/18 kg) resembles a raven. Many birds need to live near water. The blackbird enjoys a cool mountain brook, while the coastlines of northern and eastern Germany offer food and nesting places to thousands of water birds. Wetland birds like herons, ducks and geese are common, as are other waders like the common snipe. Snipe fly with a distinctive winnowing motion that produces a bleating sound from their tail feathers. For this reason its also known as the "sky goat". The great white stork, together with its dark cousin, the black stork,

builds its famous nests in eastern Germany. Further north-east, there are even a few species of nesting cranes. Most of these stay only a short time, resting before flying on further north to Scandinavia. With some luck, it might be possible to observe otters at play in north-east Germany, or even beavers, which have greatly increased in number in recent years. Their razor sharp teeth can bring down entire large

trees. Beavers use the trunk and branches to build complex dens and dams, in the process creating valuable living spaces for a wealth of other animals. Germany is also home to a unique environment, the north German mud flats. The wild North Sea recedes so far during ebb tide that several miles of the sea floor are exposed. This slick expanse is a richly laid table for coastal birds. They feast on small

crustaceans, mussels and mud worms. Flocks of swallows, seagulls and thousands of seals turn the islands and sand dunes into nurseries, while ospreys are kept busy fishing.

Mountain animals are often easily distinguished by the "alpine" prefix to their name. The alpine crow is a shy bird, now very rare. Very patient observers can spot the alpine marmot in mountain meadows. For camouflage, the alpine ptarmigan changes its feathers many times during the course of the year to match the changing colours of its environment. Golden eagles nest high in the rock walls, where ibex and chamois, champion mountain climbers, can also be found. The mountain

forests and upland moors are also home to grouse like the capercaillie. These goose-sized birds flock together in the spring at open air mating sites. The males compete for the much smaller hens with a trilling mating song.

The lynx disappeared from Europe 200 years ago, but lately the beautiful, shy wild cats are making a comeback in the Bavarian Forest.

The beaver was once common throughout Europe and Asia. Their dams and living mounds are truly remarkable constructions.

ATLANTIC OCEAN

Great Britain and Ireland

The British Isles are located in the northern Atlantic not far from the north-west coast of France. During the ice ages, the large island of Great Britain, where England, Scotland and Wales are found, was part of the European mainland.

It was only with the melting of the glaciers some 9,000 years ago that sea levels rose and what is today the English Channel filled with water. The smaller island of Ireland has been an island for a longer period of time, since approximately 11,000 years ago. Before the islands became separated from the mainland, animals and plants common in the rest of Europe migrated into these northern areas. For this reason, many species found in the British Isles today are also native to central Europe. In geological terms, the period of time since the last ice age has been short, too short to permit the development of a uniquely evolved, starkly different world of animals.

The proximity of the sea gives the British Isles a characteristically oceanic climate. This means winters are mild, but very rainy, and summers are relatively cool. The rough Scottish highlands have a climate that resembles that of the Siberian tundra. Low mosses, lichens, low grasses and scrub define the landscape. Wet, cold storm winds blow over the rocky moors even in midsummer. A few animals

0   100   200 km

1 Mole
2 Hedgehog
3 Wild rabbit
4 Hare
5 Mountain (snow) hare
6 Red squirrel
7 Grey squirrel
8 Fox
9 Badger
10 Mink
11 Otter
12 Wild cat
13 Seal
14 Right whale
15 Shetland pony
16 Red deer
17 Fallow deer
18 Sika deer
19 Roe deer
20 Muntjac
21 Wool sheep
22 Wild cattle
23 Highland cattle
24 Dartmoor pony
25 Dwarf grebe
26 Shearwater
27 Puffin
28 Northern gannet
29 Crow
30 Cormorant
31 Grey heron

The musk deer, sika deer and muntjac were introduced into England from Asia.

ENGLISH CHANNEL

found here are adapted to a tundra climate, like the snow hare or snowy owl, the latter a rare winter visitor from the far north. Animals that require a warmer, drier summer prefer the mild climate of southern England. Even the wallaby, accidentally introduced into the wild from Australia, can survive here.

Almost all the forests in the British Isles have been cleared at one time or another. The great seagoing empire needed the wood to build its ships. As a result, nearly every large forest animal – including bear, wolf, lynx and wild pig – has been gone for a long time. Deep green meadows, wild hedgerows and hilly moorlands are the distinguishing features of England, Ireland and Wales today. There are plump sheep grazing everywhere. Small forest animals like foxes, blackbirds and robins make their homes in idyllic estate parks and gardens with ancient, towering trees. The diverse species of bird living in the British Isles is world famous, including its many kinds of

native sea bird, among them the sea swallow, a variety of common tern, that flies like an arrow through the waves. The cormorant swims so deep in the water that only its head and neck are above the surface. The puffin, though actually a skilful flier and swimmer, often lands in an ungraceful belly flop. Like the guillemot, puffins nest in enormous colonies on steep cliff faces along the coast and nearby islets, where they are safe from predators. Mighty fin, humpback and right whales swim by off the coast of the small rocky islands of northern Scotland.

The British have always been passionate breeders of domestic animal species. The mighty Shire horse looks like a giant next to the tiny Shetland pony.

32 Mute swan
33 Pochard duck
34 Ring-necked duck
35 Common shelduck
36 Eider duck
37 Merganser
38 Peregrine falcon
39 Merlin
40 Scottish moorhen
41 Capercaillie (grouse)
42 Black grouse
43 Pheasant
44 Moorhen
45 Osprey
46 Woodcock
47 Curlew
48 Black-backed gull
49 Long-eared owl
50 Snowy owl
51 Barn owl
52 Kingfisher
53 Green woodpecker
54 Blackbird
55 Alpine crow
56 Raven
57 Robin
58 Monkfish
59 Torpedo fish
60 Salmon
61 Whiting
62 Atlantic cod
63 Eel
64 Sea bream
65 Catfish
66 Turbot
67 Squid
68 Mussel

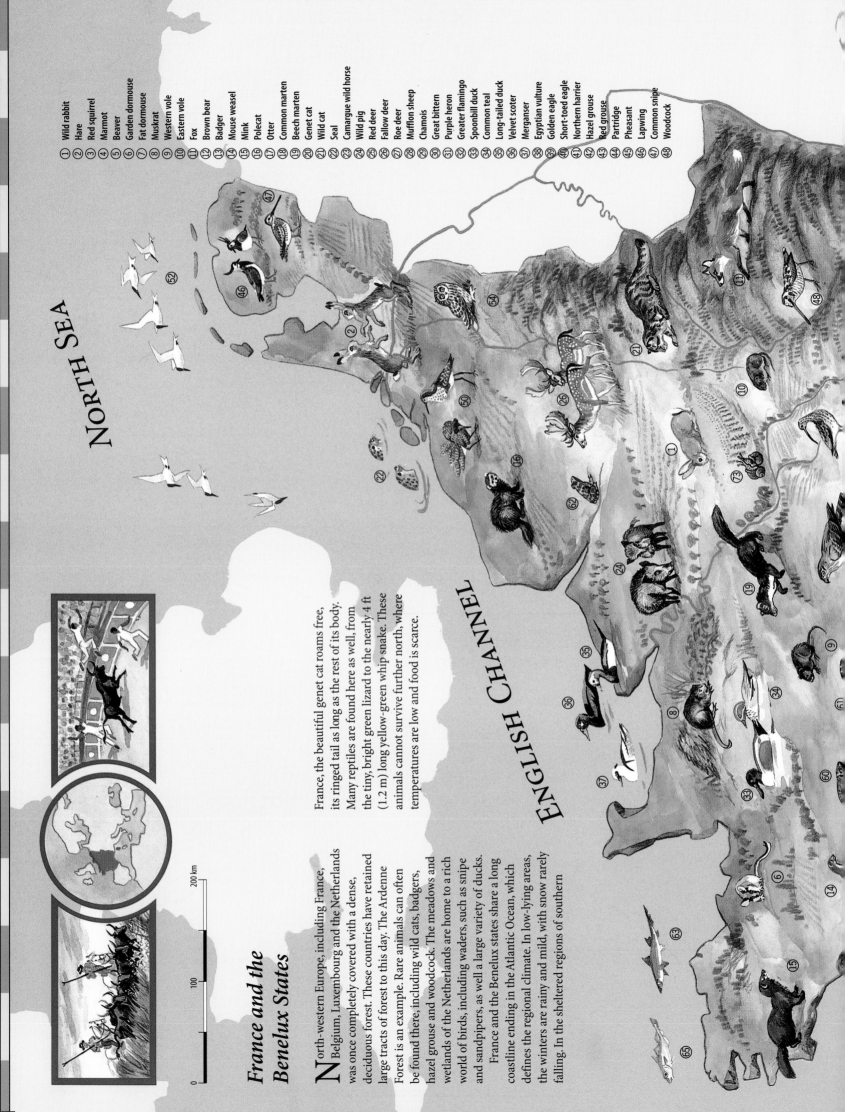

NORTH SEA

ENGLISH CHANNEL

France and the Benelux States

North-western Europe, including France, Belgium, Luxembourg and the Netherlands was once completely covered with a dense, deciduous forest. These countries have retained large tracts of forest to this day. The Ardenne Forest is an example. Rare animals can often be found there, including wild cats, badgers, hazel grouse and woodcock. The meadows and wetlands of the Netherlands are home to a rich world of birds, including waders, such as snipe and sandpipers, as well a large variety of ducks.

France and the Benelux states share a long coastline ending in the Atlantic Ocean, which defines the regional climate. In low-lying areas, the winters are rainy and mild, with snow rarely falling. In the sheltered regions of southern

France, the beautiful genet cat roams free, its ringed tail as long as the rest of its body. Many reptiles are found here as well, from the tiny, bright green lizard to the nearly 4 ft (1.2 m) long yellow-green whip snake. These animals cannot survive further north, where temperatures are low and food is scarce.

0   100   200 km

① Wild rabbit	⑰ Otter	㉝ Spoonbill duck
② Hare	⑱ Common marten	㉞ Common teal
③ Red squirrel	⑲ Beech marten	㉟ Long-tailed duck
④ Marmot	⑳ Genet cat	㊱ Velvet scoter
⑤ Beaver	㉑ Wild cat	㊲ Merganser
⑥ Garden dormouse	㉒ Seal	㊳ Egyptian vulture
⑦ Fat dormouse	㉓ Camargue wild horse	㊴ Golden eagle
⑧ Muskrat	㉔ Wild pig	㊵ Short-toed eagle
⑨ Western vole	㉕ Red deer	㊶ Northern harrier
⑩ Eastern vole	㉖ Fallow deer	㊷ Hazel grouse
⑪ Fox	㉗ Roe deer	㊸ Red grouse
⑫ Brown bear	㉘ Mufflon sheep	㊹ Partridge
⑬ Badger	㉙ Chamois	㊺ Pheasant
⑭ Mouse weasel	㉚ Great bittern	㊻ Lapwing
⑮ Mink	㉛ Purple heron	㊼ Common snipe
⑯ Polecat	㉜ Greater flamingo	㊽ Woodcock

49 Curlew
50 Ruff
51 Stone curlew
52 Common tern
53 Little owl
54 Short-eared owl
55 Spotted woodpecker
56 Woodlark
57 Wallcreeper
58 Oriole

59 Green lizard
60 Ocellated lizard
61 Yellow-green whip snake
62 Spadefoot frog
63 Smooth hound shark
64 Monkfish
65 Haddock
66 Tuna
67 Boar fish

68 Sea horse
69 Lobster
70 Starfish
71 Cicada
72 Praying mantis
73 Land snail

MEDITERRANEAN SEA

Although more common further south, the small Egyptian bearded vulture, with its wingspan of nearly 4 ft (1.2 m), can be seen soaring over the valleys of the French Pyrenees, the mountain range that separates France from Spain.

Parts of southern France lying directly on the warm Mediterranean coast are practically tropical. The extensive lowlands of the Rhone Delta, with its many lakes and saltwater lagoons, are home to the famous Camargue wild horses. This swampy landscape is an important refuge for countless numbers of water birds. Even the magnificent greater flamingo has

been seen here, at the northernmost extent of its breeding range. Together with the rare purple heron and little egret, they flock here in enormous colonies, searching with their curved beaks through the brackish water for crustaceans and other small creatures. They build their nests into odd-looking mud towers,

highly visible on the flat coastal plains. In the drier, sandy dune and steppe regions, the Camargue wild horses race across the landscape. They were once bred as robust workhorses used to herd fighting bulls destined for the ring. Today, the Camargue horses live

more or less wild in small herds consisting of a dominant stallion, his harem of mares and their foals. The stallions fight each other passionately for control of the herds. The dry grasslands are also home to other warm climate species, including the green-blue ocellated lizard, the largest and most beautiful of its kind found in Europe. Praying mantises and trilling cicadas are everywhere.

The wild mountain landscapes of the island of Corsica are home to the mufflon sheep, which came to the island as a domesticated species from the Western European mainland.

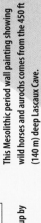

This Mesolithic period wall painting showing wild horses and aurochs comes from the 450 ft (140 m) deep Lascaux Cave.

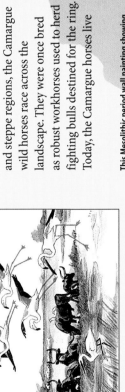

In the Camargue, the cattle egret feasts on the insects stirred up by the grazing cattle.

Spain and Portugal

Spain and Portugal are located on the Iberian Peninsula in the south-western corner of Europe. Iberia is bordered on the west by the cool Atlantic Ocean and on the east by the warm Mediterranean Sea. Here, animals that are common further north can share a habitat with animals more typical of Africa. Wolves, lynx, brown bear and wild cats have found their last refuge in the forests and inaccessible mountain peaks at the northern and southern ends of the peninsula. Genuine "southerners" are the heat-loving cattle egret, scorpions and the many native species of reptile. Among the latter is the chameleon, with eyes that can move in all directions independently of each other. Chameleons can alter their skin colour at a moment's notice. Motionless, it awaits its prey,

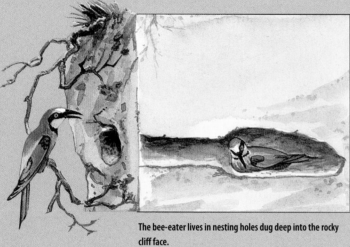

The bee-eater lives in nesting holes dug deep into the rocky cliff face.

mostly flies and other insects, until, lightning fast, its long tongue shoots out from its mouth. The African civet cat has found a home in the hot climate of Andalusia, where it hunts rats and snakes. Like the closely related mongoose, the civet cat seems to be immune to snake venom. At the southernmost tip of Iberia, a colony of Barbary apes has lived on the Rock of Gibraltar for many generations. They are the only apes native to Europe. They climb up and down the cliffs, hunting insects and foraging for plants.

Summers are hot and dry in the Meseta, the central high plains of Spain. Grasslands and cultivated fields are the dominant environment. The wide-open landscape is the ideal hunting ground for a number of predatory birds, among them the mighty Spanish imperial eagle, the smaller dwarf eagle and four different kinds of vulture. With no place to hide, non-flying birds like the great bustard can only protect themselves against these enemies via camouflage, aided by their ingenious plumage, which easily blends into the background. Southern Spain and Portugal are home to Europe's last stands of cork and stone oak forest, inhabited by the lovely European roller, also known as the almond crow. The colourful bee-eater and rarely seen black stork are also found here. Bee-eaters are birds that breed in large colonies and are skilful at snatching insects out of the air in mid-flight. Also famous for a rich bird life are the salt marshes on the western and southern coasts of the peninsula, where large areas are repeatedly flooded and re-exposed by the ebbing and flowing of the sea. This has led to an environment dotted with lagoons and swamps full of small living creatures. These are a rich source of nutrition for the nesting spoonbills and greater flamingos, as well as for the up to 30,000 cranes that migrate here from the far north every winter.

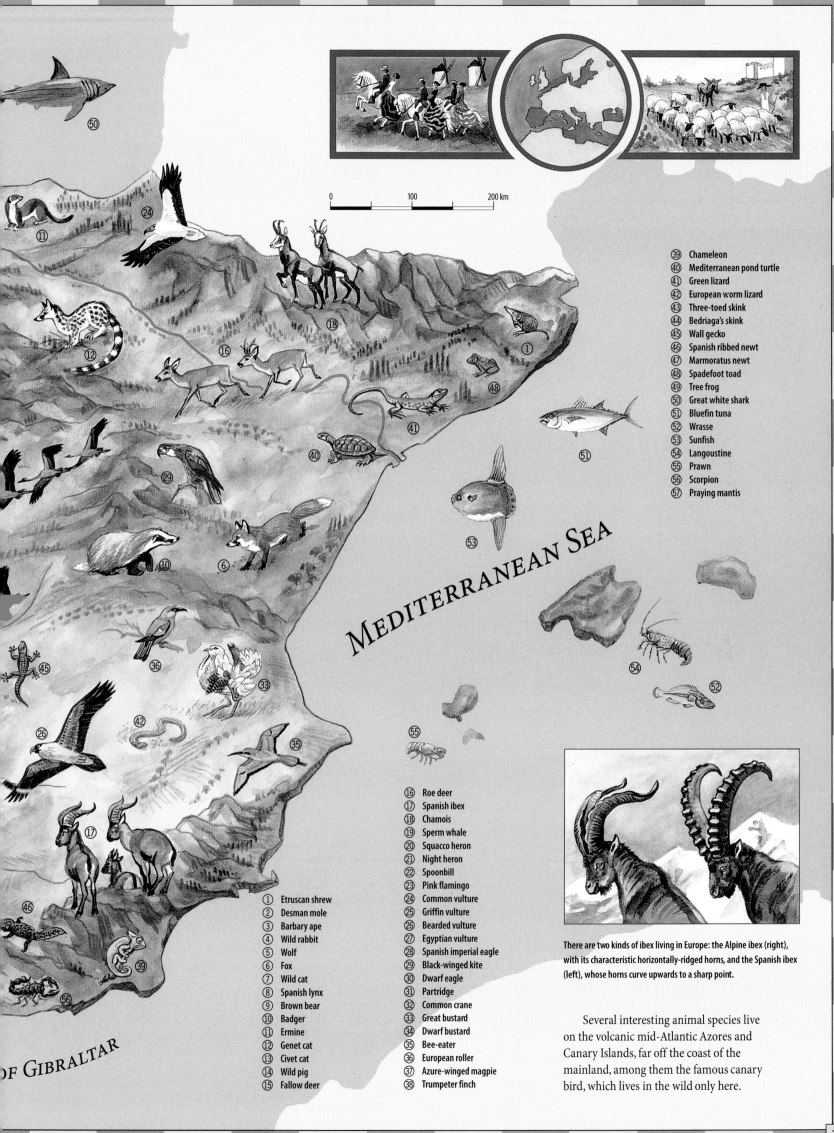

MEDITERRANEAN SEA

OF GIBRALTAR

39	Chameleon
40	Mediterranean pond turtle
41	Green lizard
42	European worm lizard
43	Three-toed skink
44	Bedriaga's skink
45	Wall gecko
46	Spanish ribbed newt
47	Marmoratus newt
48	Spadefoot toad
49	Tree frog
50	Great white shark
51	Bluefin tuna
52	Wrasse
53	Sunfish
54	Langoustine
55	Prawn
56	Scorpion
57	Praying mantis

1	Etruscan shrew
2	Desman mole
3	Barbary ape
4	Wild rabbit
5	Wolf
6	Fox
7	Wild cat
8	Spanish lynx
9	Brown bear
10	Badger
11	Ermine
12	Genet cat
13	Civet cat
14	Wild pig
15	Fallow deer

16	Roe deer
17	Spanish ibex
18	Chamois
19	Sperm whale
20	Squacco heron
21	Night heron
22	Spoonbill
23	Pink flamingo
24	Common vulture
25	Griffin vulture
26	Bearded vulture
27	Egyptian vulture
28	Spanish imperial eagle
29	Black-winged kite
30	Dwarf eagle
31	Partridge
32	Common crane
33	Great bustard
34	Dwarf bustard
35	Bee-eater
36	European roller
37	Azure-winged magpie
38	Trumpeter finch

There are two kinds of ibex living in Europe: the Alpine ibex (right), with its characteristic horizontally-ridged horns, and the Spanish ibex (left), whose horns curve upwards to a sharp point.

Several interesting animal species live on the volcanic mid-Atlantic Azores and Canary Islands, far off the coast of the mainland, among them the famous canary bird, which lives in the wild only here.

0   100   200 km

According to legend, Romulus and Remus, the twin founders of Rome, were nursed by a she-wolf.

ADRIATIC SEA

MEDITERRANEAN SEA

Italy, Greece and the Slavic States

Summers are hot and dry in the countries of the eastern Mediterranean. Winters are mild and wet. The forests that once grew here have been nearly completely cleared, mostly for shipbuilding, with a few small exceptions. Today, the landscape is dominated by olive groves, vineyards and dry shrub lands known as maquis.

This wide-open habitat is home to numerous songbirds, like the sylvia and mockingbird, which benefit from its rich insect life and sheltered nesting places. The hot summer nights are filled with the never-ending trill of the cicadas,

In Italy, the primeval-looking domestic water buffalo is a common sight. Its wild forebears came from India.

as tortoises and lizards rest on stones warmed by the Mediterranean sun. Wall geckos are frequent visitors, their gripping toes running up and down the smoothest house and garden walls with ease. Chameleons, an introduced species from Africa, are also common.

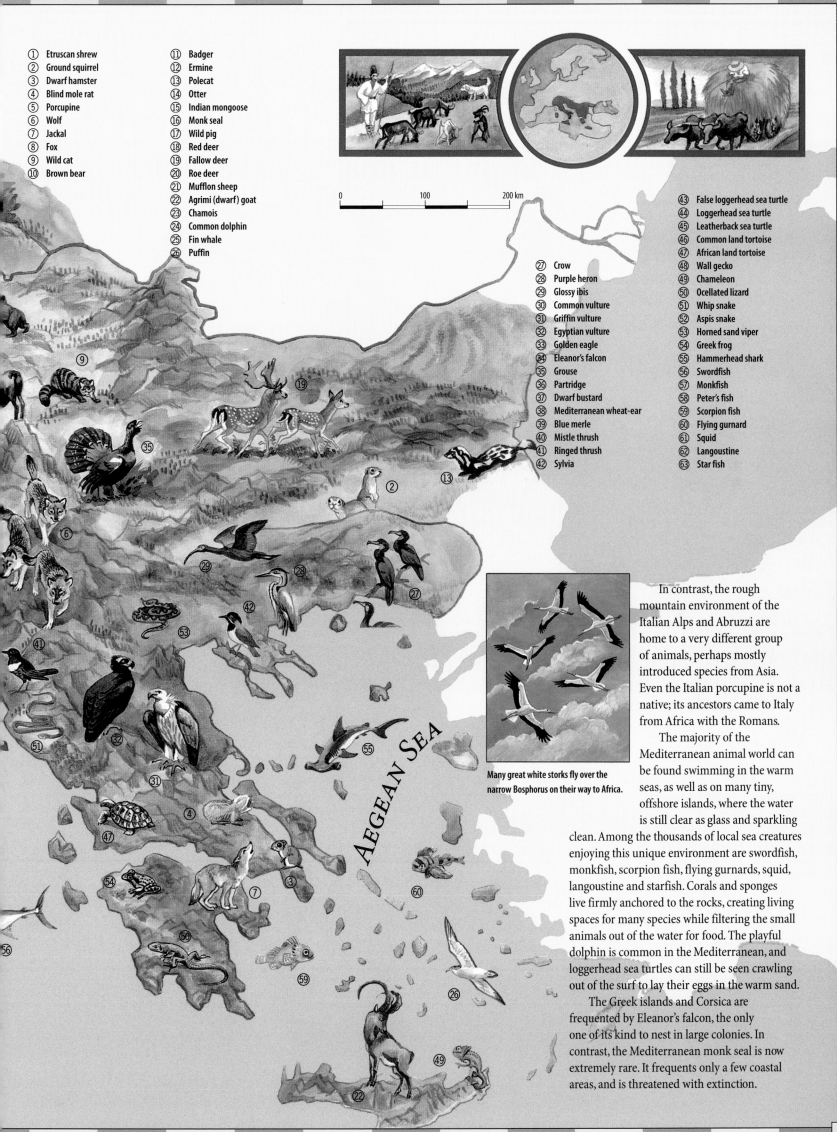

1 Etruscan shrew
2 Ground squirrel
3 Dwarf hamster
4 Blind mole rat
5 Porcupine
6 Wolf
7 Jackal
8 Fox
9 Wild cat
10 Brown bear
11 Badger
12 Ermine
13 Polecat
14 Otter
15 Indian mongoose
16 Monk seal
17 Wild pig
18 Red deer
19 Fallow deer
20 Roe deer
21 Mufflon sheep
22 Agrimi (dwarf) goat
23 Chamois
24 Common dolphin
25 Fin whale
26 Puffin

27 Crow
28 Purple heron
29 Glossy ibis
30 Common vulture
31 Griffin vulture
32 Egyptian vulture
33 Golden eagle
34 Eleanor's falcon
35 Grouse
36 Partridge
37 Dwarf bustard
38 Mediterranean wheat-ear
39 Blue merle
40 Mistle thrush
41 Ringed thrush
42 Sylvia

43 False loggerhead sea turtle
44 Loggerhead sea turtle
45 Leatherback sea turtle
46 Common land tortoise
47 African land tortoise
48 Wall gecko
49 Chameleon
50 Ocellated lizard
51 Whip snake
52 Aspis snake
53 Horned sand viper
54 Greek frog
55 Hammerhead shark
56 Swordfish
57 Monkfish
58 Peter's fish
59 Scorpion fish
60 Flying gurnard
61 Squid
62 Langoustine
63 Star fish

0   100   200 km

AEGEAN SEA

Many great white storks fly over the narrow Bosphorus on their way to Africa.

In contrast, the rough mountain environment of the Italian Alps and Abruzzi are home to a very different group of animals, perhaps mostly introduced species from Asia. Even the Italian porcupine is not a native; its ancestors came to Italy from Africa with the Romans.

The majority of the Mediterranean animal world can be found swimming in the warm seas, as well as on many tiny, offshore islands, where the water is still clear as glass and sparkling clean. Among the thousands of local sea creatures enjoying this unique environment are swordfish, monkfish, scorpion fish, flying gurnards, squid, langoustine and starfish. Corals and sponges live firmly anchored to the rocks, creating living spaces for many species while filtering the small animals out of the water for food. The playful dolphin is common in the Mediterranean, and loggerhead sea turtles can still be seen crawling out of the surf to lay their eggs in the warm sand.

The Greek islands and Corsica are frequented by Eleanor's falcon, the only one of its kind to nest in large colonies. In contrast, the Mediterranean monk seal is now extremely rare. It frequents only a few coastal areas, and is threatened with extinction.

NORWEGIAN SEA

NORTH SEA

27 Walrus
28 Lemming
29 Bottle-nosed dolphin
30 Humpbacked whale
31 Elk (Moose)
32 Reindeer
33 Roe deer
34 Musk ox
35 Arctic loon
36 Trumpeter swan
37 Canadian goose
38 Long-tailed duck
39 Sea eagle
40 Osprey
41 Marsh harrier

1 Norwegian brown bat
2 Least shrew
3 Mole
4 Hedgehog
5 Wild rabbit
6 Hare
7 Red squirrel
8 Flying squirrel
9 Beaver
10 Muskrat
11 Lemming
12 Wolf
13 Fox

0   200   400 km

The volcanic island of Iceland is famous for its wide variety of bird species. Puffins, long-tailed duck and the common murre (guillemot) dive from its cliffs seeking food for themselves and their young.

BALTIC SEA

Scandinavia

Scandinavia lies in the icy far north of Europe, so far north that parts of it lie within the Arctic Circle. The fish-rich coastal regions of Norway are home to a typically arctic range of animals, including the walrus, polar bear and several species of seal. Further south, extensive deciduous and mixed pine forests, rugged mountain ranges and large lake districts offer a range of exceptionally diverse habitats, including forested taiga and bare, grassy tundra.

The lynx, wolf and wolverine wander through the forests searching for prey. The powerful, fearless wolverine is known as the "glutton" in the native Scandinavian languages, a name it carries not because it eats more than other animals, but because the word for glutton in Norwegian sounds like the word "fjellfoss", which means "mountain cat". It is even still possible to meet a brown bear in the wild here. Every year, thousands of salmon swim upstream returning to the rivers of their birth to lay their own eggs. They leap some 10 ft (3 m) in the air against the current, covering a distance of 20 ft (6 m) with one jump. After laying their eggs, they return to the sea. Life is hard during the cold, long northern winter. In the spring, cranes and wading birds like the sandpiper, as well as many other species of bird, return to Scandinavia from their winter migration to the warm south, flying across the European mainland to Africa and the Mediterranean regions. The larger inhabitants of the taiga and tundra are better adapted to the difficult climate. The mighty elk strides through the snow on its long legs, while the patient reindeer searches beneath the snow for lichens and roots. Great herds of reindeer cross into the tundra regions during the summer; for the winter, the forested taiga provides more nutrition and protection. The Laplanders, members of the Sami indigenous group living in the north of Norway, Sweden and Finland, domesticated the reindeer many centuries ago. Even today, the Sami nomadically follow the herds back and forth. Reindeer provide them with meat, milk, leather and fur, as well as being strong work and transportation animals. Sixty years ago, the primeval-looking musk ox was reintroduced in Scandinavia. Long extinct on the continent, they once roamed across the whole of Europe.

The plumage of the ptarmigan changes twice a year, the number of times that the seasons change in the tundra. It is as well camouflaged in its snow-white winter feathers as it is in the summer, when its plumage is a variegated brown. Many predators, like the arctic fox and ermine, find them nevertheless.

The tiny lemmings are a tundra species. They pass the cold winter months in well-designed tunnels dug deep under the thick snow.

14 Arctic fox
15 Marten
16 Polar bear
17 Brown bear
18 Wolverine
19 Ermine
20 Marten
21 Sable
22 Otter
23 Lynx
24 Sea lion
25 Ringed seal
26 Grey seal

42 Gyrfalcon
43 Ptarmigan
44 Moorhen
45 Grouse
46 Crane
47 Oystercatcher
48 Golden plover
49 Sandpiper
50 Northern (red-necked) phalarope
51 Arctic skua
52 Caspian tern
53 Herring gull
54 Lesser auk
55 Guillemot (common murre)
56 Dovekie
57 Black Guillemot
58 Puffin
59 Eurasian collared dove

60 Pygmy owl
61 Eagle owl
62 Snowy owl
63 Ural owl
64 Northern hawk owl
65 Black woodpecker
66 Nutcracker
67 Raven
68 Waxwing
69 Common crossbill
70 Siberian tit
71 Goldcrest
72 Sea lamprey
73 Porbeagle (shark)
74 Common eel
75 Conger eel
76 Herring
77 Salmon

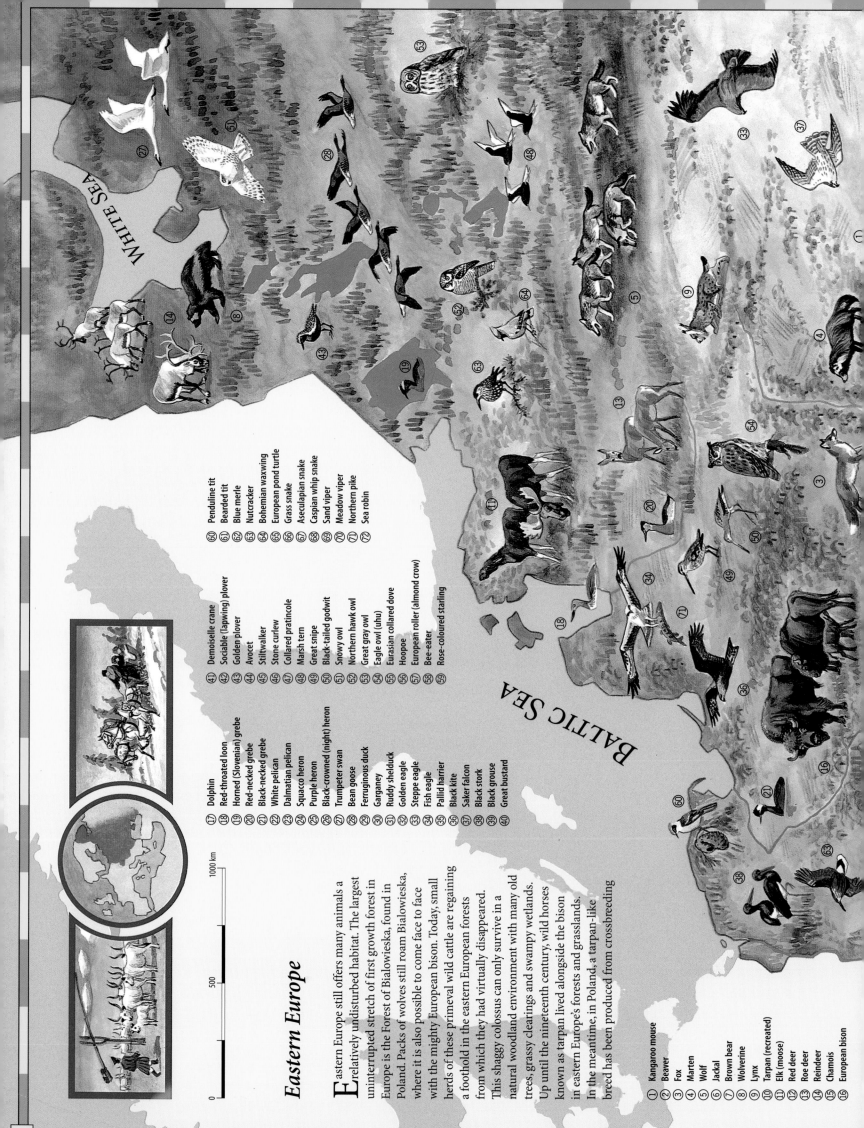

Eastern Europe

Eastern Europe still offers many animals a relatively undisturbed habitat. The largest uninterrupted stretch of first growth forest in Europe is the Forest of Bialowieska, found in Poland. Packs of wolves still roam Bialowieska, where it is also possible to come face to face with the mighty European bison. Today, small herds of these primeval wild cattle are regaining a foothold in the eastern European forests from which they had virtually disappeared. This shaggy colossus can only survive in a natural woodland environment with many old trees, grassy clearings and swampy wetlands. Up until the nineteenth century, wild horses known as tarpan lived alongside the bison in eastern Europe's forests and grasslands. In the meantime, in Poland, a tarpan-like breed has been produced from crossbreeding

BALTIC SEA

0   500   1000 km

① Kangaroo mouse
② Beaver
③ Fox
④ Marten
⑤ Wolf
⑥ Jackal
⑦ Brown bear
⑧ Wolverine
⑨ Lynx
⑩ Tarpan (recreated)
⑪ Elk (moose)
⑫ Red deer
⑬ Roe deer
⑭ Reindeer
⑮ Chamois
⑯ European bison

⑰ Dolphin
⑱ Red-throated loon
⑲ Horned (Slovenian) grebe
⑳ Red-necked grebe
㉑ Black-necked grebe
㉒ White pelican
㉓ Dalmatian pelican
㉔ Squacco heron
㉕ Purple heron
㉖ Black-crowned (night) heron
㉗ Trumpeter swan
㉘ Bean goose
㉙ Ferruginous duck
㉚ Garganey
㉛ Ruddy shelduck
㉜ Golden eagle
㉝ Steppe eagle
㉞ Fish eagle
㉟ Pallid harrier
㊱ Black kite
㊲ Saker falcon
㊳ Black stork
㊴ Black grouse
㊵ Great bustard

㊶ Demoiselle crane
㊷ Sociable (lapwing) plover
㊸ Golden plover
㊹ Avocet
㊺ Stiltwalker
㊻ Stone curlew
㊼ Collared pratincole
㊽ Marsh tern
㊾ Great snipe
㊿ Black-tailed godwit
51 Snowy owl
52 Northern hawk owl
53 Great gray owl
54 Eagle owl (uhu)
55 Eurasian collared dove
56 Hoopoe
57 European roller (almond crow)
58 Bee-eater
59 Rose-coloured starling

60 Penduline tit
61 Bearded tit
62 Blue merle
63 Nutcracker
64 Bohemian waxwing
66 European pond turtle
66 Grass snake
67 Aesculapian snake
68 Caspian whip snake
69 Sand viper
70 Meadow viper
71 Northern pike
72 Sea robin

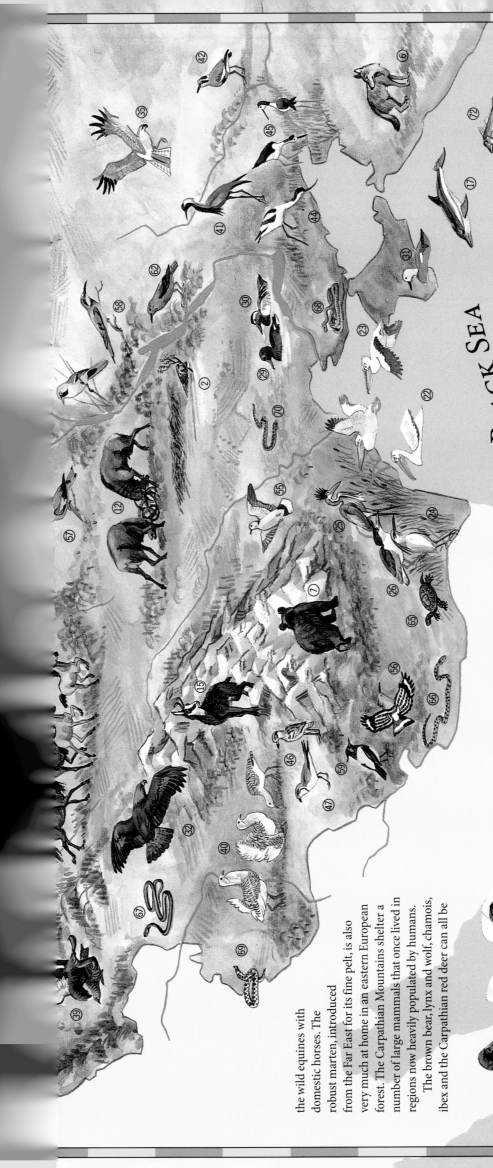

the wild equines with domestic horses. The robust marten, introduced from the Far East for its fine pelt, is also very much at home in an eastern European forest. The Carpathian Mountains shelter a number of large mammals that once lived in regions now heavily populated by humans.

The brown bear, lynx and wolf, chamois, ibex and the Carpathian red deer can all be

Two species of pelican live in the delta of the Danube River. Nestlings eat their meals directly out of the beak pouch of their parents.

found there. At high altitudes, above the tree line, the social marmots live exactly as they do in the Alps, passing the winter in well-sheltered dens dug into the earth. They only emerge after the first spring sun has completely melted the snow cover. With giant appetites they feed off the rich mountain grasses and herbs. For some of the other animal species, the Carpathian Mountains are a natural boundary. Field mice, for example, are not found east of that mountain range. The central lowlands of

Eastern Europe are defined by treeless steppe stretching for thousands of miles to the east. The steppe is where the continental climate predominates. The summers are dry and hot, with cold winters, during which icy cold winds blow over the snow-covered plains. Steppe grasses and herbs support a wide variety of rodent species, such as ground squirrels and hamsters, who put away a large store of seeds and nuts for the long winters. Predatory birds, such as the golden eagle and small saker falcon, swoop through the skies hunting them down, their astoundingly sharp vision letting them spot their prey scurrying across the wide-open landscape from a mile or more away.

The kangaroo mouse is another typical steppe animal. With its long rear legs, it can

jump as far as 7 ft (2 m), despite being only 6 in (15 cm) long. In the transitional area where the steppe borders on woodlands, the colourful bee-eater skillfully snatches insects in full flight out of the air. The Danube basin on the Black Sea is a broad delta with low-forested islands where the scrub reaches 15 ft (4 m)

in height. It is home to countless numbers of water birds. Cormorants and many species of heron fish in its waters, plucking small animals from its nutrient-rich mud flats. Snakes and turtles lie hidden in the thick reeds. In contrast to near relatives on land, the pond turtle is a slick hunter, specialising in fish, frogs and water insects. Sadly, the animal paradise of the Danube Delta is now considered one of the most threatened wetland environments on earth.

Askania Nova is a zoological research farm in the southern Ukraine. All varieties of steppe, grassland and savannah animals are bred here.

BLACK SEA

Northern and Central Asia

Northern and Central Asia cover an enormous area of land, reaching from the arctic tundra in the north to the tropical coral reefs of the South China Sea. It includes so many different climate zones that northlanders like the polar bear and walrus are present along with great apes and sea snakes.

During the short summers, the treeless tundra virtually teems with animals. Year round inhabitants include the mountain hare, also known as the snow hare, along with a number of predatory birds that hunt small animals. Migratory birds, such as the snow goose and Canadian goose, are also present in large numbers. The tender meadow herbs and masses of insects are what attract them. Other animal species prefer the broad forested region known as the taiga, as well as the deciduous forests further south. Elk and deer feast on the plant life, but must take care not to be stalked by hungry wolves during the snowy winter months. Wolves hunting in packs can easily bring down a large herbivore. Further to the east, the mighty Siberian tiger is the primary predator, although increasingly rare in its natural habitat. Smaller hunters like the sable, marten and polecat prey on birds and rodents. The sable lives in the wild today under strong protection. Its magnificent – and valuable – pelt had led to its being hunted nearly to extinction. Further to the south, the great grassy steppes that were also a feature of eastern Europe define yet another series of animal habitats. The industrious ground squirrel, so common further west, stops here twice a year in order to hibernate, spending the hottest part of the summer and deepest cold of the winter in well-constructed dens dug deep into the earth. When they are not sleeping, these small squirrels are very alert and always on the look out, standing tall on their hind legs, suspiciously scanning the horizon for predators. At the first sign of danger the entire colony disappears underground in the blink of an eye. Perhaps the ground squirrels have spotted a wandering herd of Saiga antelope. These nervous animals with their enormous, bulbous snouts are extraordinarily hardy and adaptive to a variety of conditions. They can survive the tremendous cold of the winter as well as summer's devastating sandstorms.

Recently reintroduced, the small, sturdy Przewalski's horse, the last surviving wild ancestor of the domestic horse, thrives on the Mongolian steppe. The barren Gobi Desert borders this steppe on all sides. The Gobi is the home of the last two-humped wild camels as well as the domesticated pack camel bred from them.

The cool mountain slopes of the Himalayas are grassy enough for well-adapted herd animals. The high plains of Tibet are home to the kiang, a wild ass, and the famous yak, both comfortable at altitudes of 13,000–19,500 ft (4,000–6,000 m). They have somehow adapted to the hard life of icy, thin, oxygen-poor air and meagre forage. The primeval Yak, a variety of wild cattle, has a particularly striking, long, hairy coat. Matted like felt, it keeps the animal warm even during the coldest part of a Himalayan winter. Tibet is also home to a large wild sheep, the argali, which has horns that can grow to over 3 ft (1 m) in length. At the highest altitudes on earth, where the mountain

The Pere David's deer has completely died out in the central Asian wetlands. There are plans today to reintroduce it in its original habitat.

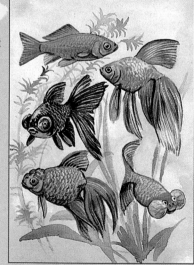

The Chinese have been breeding goldfish for ornamental ponds and aquaria for the past 1,000 years. Today, more than 100 different species are recognized.

① Golden snub-nosed monkey	⑨ Arctic fox
② Red-faced macaque	⑩ Wolf
③ Himalayan pika	⑪ Brown bear
④ Mountain (snow) hare	⑫ Kamschatka bear
⑤ Beaver	⑬ Polar bear
⑥ Sable	⑭ Asiatic black (collared) bear
⑦ Steppe marmot	⑮ Greater panda bear
⑧ Korsak fox	⑯ Lesser panda bear

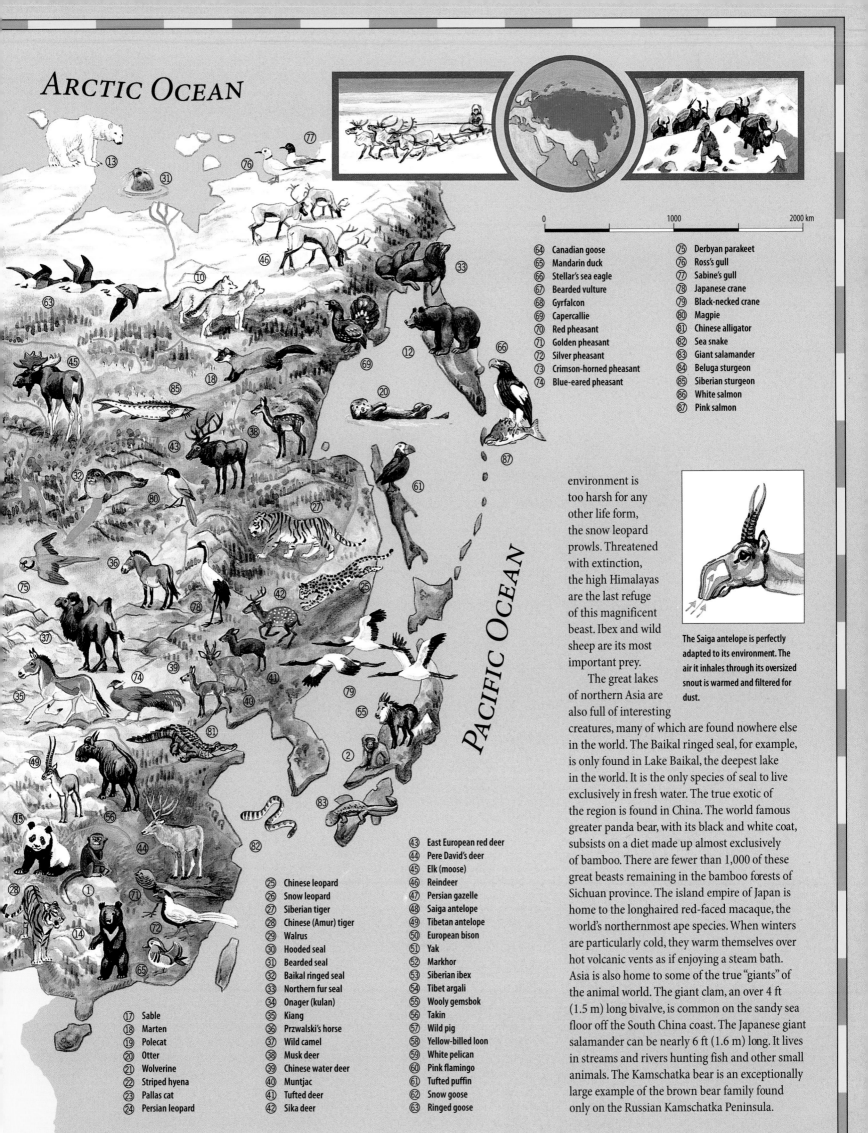

ARCTIC OCEAN

PACIFIC OCEAN

Scale bar: 0 — 1000 — 2000 km

Legend

64 Canadian goose
65 Mandarin duck
66 Stellar's sea eagle
67 Bearded vulture
68 Gyrfalcon
69 Capercallie
70 Red pheasant
71 Golden pheasant
72 Silver pheasant
73 Crimson-horned pheasant
74 Blue-eared pheasant

75 Derbyan parakeet
76 Ross's gull
77 Sabine's gull
78 Japanese crane
79 Black-necked crane
80 Magpie
81 Chinese alligator
82 Sea snake
83 Giant salamander
84 Beluga sturgeon
85 Siberian sturgeon
86 White salmon
87 Pink salmon

17 Sable
18 Marten
19 Polecat
20 Otter
21 Wolverine
22 Striped hyena
23 Pallas cat
24 Persian leopard

25 Chinese leopard
26 Snow leopard
27 Siberian tiger
28 Chinese (Amur) tiger
29 Walrus
30 Hooded seal
31 Bearded seal
32 Baikal ringed seal
33 Northern fur seal
34 Onager (kulan)
35 Kiang
36 Przwalski's horse
37 Wild camel
38 Musk deer
39 Chinese water deer
40 Muntjac
41 Tufted deer
42 Sika deer

43 East European red deer
44 Pere David's deer
45 Elk (moose)
46 Reindeer
47 Persian gazelle
48 Saiga antelope
49 Tibetan antelope
50 European bison
51 Yak
52 Markhor
53 Siberian ibex
54 Tibet argali
55 Wooly gemsbok
56 Takin
57 Wild pig
58 Yellow-billed loon
59 White pelican
60 Pink flamingo
61 Tufted puffin
62 Snow goose
63 Ringed goose

The Saiga antelope is perfectly adapted to its environment. The air it inhales through its oversized snout is warmed and filtered for dust.

environment is too harsh for any other life form, the snow leopard prowls. Threatened with extinction, the high Himalayas are the last refuge of this magnificent beast. Ibex and wild sheep are its most important prey.

The great lakes of northern Asia are also full of interesting creatures, many of which are found nowhere else in the world. The Baikal ringed seal, for example, is only found in Lake Baikal, the deepest lake in the world. It is the only species of seal to live exclusively in fresh water. The true exotic of the region is found in China. The world famous greater panda bear, with its black and white coat, subsists on a diet made up almost exclusively of bamboo. There are fewer than 1,000 of these great beasts remaining in the bamboo forests of Sichuan province. The island empire of Japan is home to the longhaired red-faced macaque, the world's northernmost ape species. When winters are particularly cold, they warm themselves over hot volcanic vents as if enjoying a steam bath. Asia is also home to some of the true "giants" of the animal world. The giant clam, an over 4 ft (1.5 m) long bivalve, is common on the sandy sea floor off the South China coast. The Japanese giant salamander can be nearly 6 ft (1.6 m) long. It lives in streams and rivers hunting fish and other small animals. The Kamschatka bear is an exceptionally large example of the brown bear family found only on the Russian Kamschatka Peninsula.

1 Platypus
2 Long-nosed echidna
3 Short-nosed echidna
4 Langier
5 Quoll cat
6 Numbat
7 Tasmanian devil
8 Marsupial mole
9 Opossum
10 Greater sugar glider
11 Leadbeater's possum
12 Brushtail possum
13 Koala
14 Phalanger
15 Wombat
16 Wallaby
17 Quokka
18 Wallaroo
19 Red kangaroo
20 Colugo
21 Slow loris
22 Tarsis
23 Cynomolgus monkey

24 Proboscis monkey
25 Crested gibbon
26 Lar gibbon
27 Siamang gibbon
28 Orang-utan
29 Fossa
30 Sun bear
31 Clouded leopard
32 Bengal tiger
33 Sumatran tiger
34 Australian sea lion
35 Asiatic elephant
36 Malayan tapir
37 Sumatran rhinoceros
38 Javan rhinoceros
39 Babirusa
40 Mouse deer
41 Gaur

INDIAN OCEAN

SOUTH CHINA SEA

South-east Asia, New Guinea, Australia and New Zealand

The climate of the tropical rainforests of South-east Asia is hot, humid and wet. Tigers, leopards, elephants and rhinoceros wander through the dense forests and grassy clearings. High above in the forest canopy a wide variety of monkeys and apes swing through the branches, from the small tarsiers, a variety of prosimian, to the giant orang-utans, a great ape that today can only be found on the Indonesian islands of Borneo and Sumatra. The proboscis money and slender gibbons are also native to South-east Asia. Rhinoceros hornbills fight small arboreal apes for tasty tropical fruits growing high in the

Compass termites build nests that are over 10 ft (3 m) tall and always oriented in a north-south direction.

Dingoes introduced some 4,000 years ago by migrating humans quickly drove many of Australia's native predators, like this Tasmanian tiger, away from the continent.

trees. Frogs and colugos, the latter a lemur-like animal that uses its thin flying membranes as parachutes, soar through the air between trees.

Like an invisible boundary, the Wallace line east of Java, Borneo and the Philippines separates the Asian from the Australian animal worlds. The Australian continent drifted away from the Asian land mass some 40 million years ago, well before most of today's mammal species evolved. What Australia has instead are marsupials.

Marsupials also produce milk for their young, but carry them inside their bodies for only a short period of time. After their birth, the tiny, helpless babies must live for an extended period inside

- Banteng
- Tamarau
- Anoa
- Japanese serow
- Southern cassowary
- Northern cassowary
- Emu
- Kiwi
- Little penguin
- Australian pelican
- Black swan
- Magpie goose
- Cape Barren goose
- Philippine eagle
- White-bellied sea eagle
- Brush turkey
- Red junglefowl
- Takahe
- Crowned pigeon
- Salmon-crested cockatoo

62 Long-billed corella
63 Mitchell's cockatoo
64 Sulphur-crested cockatoo
65 Palm cockatoo
66 Pink cockatoo
67 Eclectus parrot
68 Blue-headed racquet tail
69 Cockatiel
70 Parakeet
71 Kea
72 Tawny frogmouth
73 Kookaburra
74 Great pied hornbill
75 Lyre tail
76 Satin bowerbird
77 Golden bowerbird
78 Great bird of paradise
79 Blue bird of paradise
80 Snake-necked turtle
81 Saltwater crocodile

82 False gavial
83 Komodo dragon
84 Lace monitor
85 Tuatara
86 Thorny devil
87 Reticulated python
88 Black-headed python
89 Death adder
90 Propelodytes wagneri

91 Malayan horned frog
92 Gliding tree frog
93 Australian lungfish
94 Butterfly fish
95 Moray eel
96 Sea snake
97 Hawksbill turtle
98 Wallaby

0   500   1000   1500 km

Introduced by European settlers, the wild rabbit population has grown to plague proportions in Australia, a veritable feast for the native wedge-tailed eagle.

the mother's pouch. Marsupials have adapted to every one of Australia's many habitats. Koalas dominate the eucalyptus forests to the east, while the giant red kangaroo reigns over the central dry zone and wallabies hop through the tropical rainforests of the north-east and the island of New Guinea. Even the echidna, one of the most primitive marsupials, has survived until today, as has the platypus, the only mammal that lays eggs.

In the bird world, the ancestors of the cockatoo, bird of paradise, flightless cassowary and emu migrated here from very far away.

A special natural treasure is Australia's Great Barrier Reef off the north-east coast, a one-of-a-kind underwater paradise. Further east in the Pacific Ocean lie the islands that make up New Zealand. On the still heavily forested northern island a very ancient species of lizard still survives: the tuatara. It has a third eye right in the middle of its forehead. New Zealand is also home to the kiwi bird, with its hair-like feathers, and the playful kea parrot.

The colourful zebra finch is a popular pet.

PACIFIC OCEAN

We only see parakeets when they are in a cage, but in their natural habitat they fly and roost in enormous colonies covering the landscape.

Western and Southern Asia

Western Asia has a subtropical climate. Its proximity to the tropical zone means that the weather is warm, but lacking the moisture of the rainforests. The lack of water and dehydrating effect of the hot sun are the biggest challenges for the animals that live here. The Arabian Peninsula consists almost entirely of sandy desert and scrublands where almost nothing can grow. Large herbivores like the oryx and elegant gazelle have to be constantly on the move searching for food and water. Further to the east, on the dry plains of Iran, the onager, an ancient wild ass, still roams free.

In India, macaques are considered sacred. They live undisturbed, and well-fed, in temples and villages.

But most desert animals are much smaller. Unlike the large hoofed animals, they can hide during the day under rocks or in burrows deep in the ground. They come out only as the hot sun is setting. Dusk is the time when the desert truly comes alive. The desert lynx, also known as the caracal, as well as its much smaller relative, the sand cat, are well adapted to the dry environment. Both can live almost entirely without access to running water. They get all the moisture they need from their prey. In addition, the sand cat has small hairs on the underside of its paws to protect its feet from the hot sand. Both the striped African desert cat and feral domestic cats can survive in the dry scrublands that are only a little less arid than the sand desert.

For almost 400 different species of beetle, scorpions and other burrowing insects, the desert is a kind of paradise. One of the most famous beetle varieties is the dung, or scarab beetle, revered as a sacred animal by the ancient Egyptians. It collects dung, which it rolls into balls, pushes along and eventually buries for future use either as a food source or a place to lay their eggs. The Arabian Desert is also home to the one-humped dromedary camel,

without which humans could not survive in the vast wastes. As wild creatures, however, these ships of the desert are no more. The species has long been completely domesticated.

Further north the climate is not as dry. There are green river valleys, lakes and forests, and more mountainous western regions. The black and white striped polecat lives here, as do porcupines and many different species of snakes, lizards and turtles. The most rare bird in the region is the hermit ibis, also known as the bald ibis, a bare headed relative of the stork.

RED SEA

1	Temple macaque	10	Jackal
2	Lion-tailed macaque	11	Fenece fox
3	Rhesus monkey	12	Sand fox
4	Desert hare	13	Afghan fox
5	Porcupine	14	African polecat
6	Jerboa	15	Striped hyena
7	Spiny mouse	16	Himalayan brown bear
8	Gerbil	17	Sloth bear
9	Kangaroo mouse	18	Mungo
		19	Sand cat

20	African desert cat	37	Hog deer
21	Swamp lynx	38	Mesopotamian fallow deer
22	Caracal	39	Gaur
23	Persian leopard	40	Water buffalo
24	Indian leopard	41	Four –horned antelope
25	Caspian tiger	42	Nilgai antelope
26	Bengal tiger	43	Indian gazelle
27	Asiatic lion	44	Persian gazelle
28	Asiatic elephant	45	Mountain gazelle
29	Hyrax	46	Blackbuck
30	Indian rhinoceros	47	Oryx
31	Onager	48	Armenian mufflon
32	Wild pig	49	Afghan urial
33	Muntiak deer	50	Wild goat
34	Chital deer	51	Ganges river dolphin
35	Sambar deer	52	Bryde's whale
36	Barasingha deer	53	Bengal vulture
		54	Pondicherry vulture
		55	Saker falcon

56. Hermit (northern bald) ibis
57. Painted stork
58. Openbill stork
59. Common peafowl
60. Sarus crane
61. Houbara bustard
62. Pin-tailed sand grouse
63. European roller
64. Rosy starling
65. Moorish tortoise
66. Swamp crocodile
67. Saltwater crocodile
68. Ganges gavial
69. King snake
70. Rattlesnake
71. Sandfish skink
72. Monitor lizard
73. Saw-scaled viper
74. Horned viper

75. Cobra
76. Blue shark
77. Coral reef fish
78. Clownfish
79. Tuna
80. Dung (Scarab) beetle

0   500   1000 km

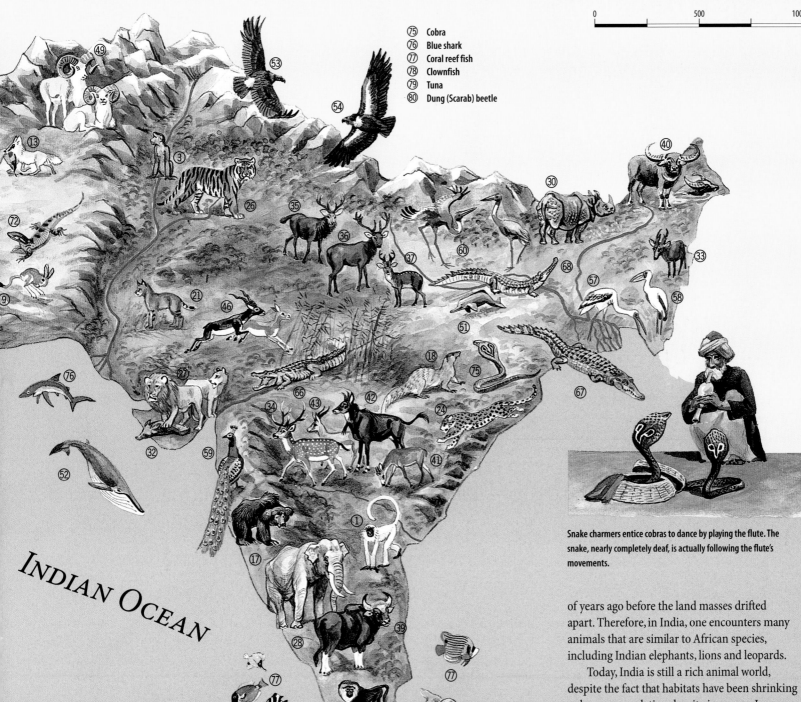

INDIAN OCEAN

Snake charmers entice cobras to dance by playing the flute. The snake, nearly completely deaf, is actually following the flute's movements.

A wide variety of animals live amid the coral reefs beneath the warm waters of the Red Sea, among them anemones, clownfish, starfish and many other colourful sea creatures.

As was the case for the Arabian Peninsula, the Indian subcontinent was joined to Africa many millions

This statue of the elephant god Ganesh illustrates the high esteem in which Hindus hold this noble beast. Ganesh is the god of wisdom and happiness.

of years ago before the land masses drifted apart. Therefore, in India, one encounters many animals that are similar to African species, including Indian elephants, lions and leopards.

Today, India is still a rich animal world, despite the fact that habitats have been shrinking as human population density increases. Large mammals like the Bengal tiger, Indian rhinoceros and Asiatic elephant survive in the wild only in small, protected areas of forest and grassland. Some animals native to the wetland regions are also threatened with extinction, the Ganges gavial for example. This reptile's long, narrow mouth can have as many as 100 teeth, which helps it catch slippery fish. The much plumper, up to 30 ft (9 m) long saltwater crocodile prefers coastal waters. The painted stork can also be found there, famous for its colourful plumage, as its name suggests, and extraordinary appetite.

Africa

Desert, savannah and rainforest are Africa's three most important environmental zones. The unbearably hot sun burns all day in the Sahara region, the largest continuous desert on earth. Rocky outcrops, the thin vegetation of the bordering Sahel, and barren sand dunes define the harsh landscape. The survival artists of the African desert include the Sahara gazelle, the small ungulate hyrax and the desert fox, also known as the fennec fox. The latter extends its enormous ears so as to catch the dry desert wind, reducing its body temperature. Better living conditions can be found in

The rock hard termite mounds, several feet tall, enclose a gigantic labyrinth of chambers and passageways kept at a constant temperature and humidity by means of an elaborate climate control system.

MEDITERRANEAN SEA

RED SEA

ATLANTIC OCEAN

1500 km
1000
500
0

① Aye-aye
② Vari
③ Sifaka lemur
④ Ring-tailed lemur
⑤ Galago
⑥ Potto
⑦ DeBrazza's monkey

⑩ Mandrill
⑪ Hamadryas baboon
⑫ Chacma baboon
⑬ Barbary ape
⑭ Chimpanzee
⑮ Lowland gorilla
⑯ Mountain gorilla
⑰ Elephant shrew
⑱ Pangolin
⑲ African ground squirrel
⑳ Fennec fox
㉑ Jackal
㉒ Bat-eared fox
㉓ African wild dog
㉔ Hyena
㉕ Aardvark
㉖ Meerkat

㉗ Genet cat
㉘ Civet cat
㉙ Fossa
㉚ Caracal
㉛ Leopard
㉜ Lion
㉝ Cheetah
㉞ South African fur seal
㉟ Ant bear
㊱ Forest elephant
㊲ Savannah elephant
㊳ Hyrax
㊴ West Indian manatee
㊵ White rhinoceros
㊶ Black rhinoceros
㊷ Wild ass
㊸ Grevy's zebra

34

the wetlands like the Nile River valley and the southern Sudan. Crocodiles, hippopotami and water birds like the rare shoebill and African fish eagle are found. South of the Sahara, the rainforest belt runs east-west straight across central Africa. The smaller forest elephant, pygmy hippopotamus and shy okapi, a short-necked forest giraffe, make these forests their home. Chimpanzees and gorillas, our nearest relatives in the animal kingdom, also favour the rainforest. The most famous African habitat is the savannah. The savannah consists of virtually uninterrupted, flat grassland scattered with acacia trees, interspersed with waterholes and swampy wetlands. Here as well, the daylight hours are brutally hot. Many parts of the savannah have a long dry season during which nearly all plant life shrivels from lack of moisture. Yet there is nowhere else on earth with so great a variety of large mammals. Enormous herds of zebra, gnu, Cape buffalo, antelope and gazelle wander across the wide plains searching for grazing land and water, trailed by a host of predators, including lions, hyenas, leopards and cheetah. Vultures circle in the air above, waiting for the kill. Only the largest land animal of all, the giant African savannah elephant, has little to fear from the predators. There are also

One of the most dangerous animals in Africa is the tiny tse-tse fly. One bite can bring on the dreaded sleeping sickness, a devastating illness that can kill.

smaller animals on the savannah, such as the long-legged secretary bird and social meerkats, the latter standing straight up in front of its den scanning the horizon for danger. The island of Madagascar has a particularly unique range of animal species, a result of its having drifted away from the African mainland some 280 million years ago. At some point in time, lemurs from the mainland made their way to the island. In other parts of the world these ancient prosimians have barely managed to survive, but

on Madagascar, isolated from large predators, they have flourished. The coelacanth, an ancient fish long thought to be extinct, was found in deep waters off the African coast. The nearest relatives of this four-finned fish left the sea for land many millions of years ago, the forefathers of all amphibians, reptiles, birds and mammals.

The small fennec fox, also known as the desert fox, hunts throughout the cold desert night, putting its thick fur coat to good use.

44 Quagga (extinct)
45 Warthog
46 Bush pig
47 Pygmy hippopotamus
48 Hippopotamus
49 Okapi
50 Giraffe
51 Cape buffalo
52 Duiker
53 Sable-backed duiker
54 Klippspringer antelope
55 Bongo
56 Greater kudu
57 Bushbuck
58 Eland
59 Giant eland
60 Sable antelope
61 Addax antelope
62 Oryx
63 Waterbuck
64 Roan antelope
65 Sable-backed antelope
66 Bontebok
67 Blesbok
68 Hartebeest
69 Wildebeest
70 Springbok
71 Sahara gazelle
72 Thomson's gazelle
73 Gerenuk gazelle
74 Nubian ibex
75 Aoudad sheep
76 African penguin
77 Ostrich

78 White pelican
79 Shoebill
80 Marabou stork
81 Ibis
82 African skimmer
83 Greater flamingo
84 Lesser flamingo
85 Nile goose
86 African fish eagle
87 Secretary bird
88 Ruppell's vulture
89 Pondicherry vulture
90 Helmeted guineafowl
91 African grey parrot
92 Giant African (Aldabra) tortoise
93 Nile crocodile

94 Nile monitor lizard
95 King python
96 Rhinoceros viper
97 Horned viper
98 Puff adder
99 Mamba
100 African lungfish
101 Coelacanth
102 Nile perch
103 Goliath beetle
104 Locust
105 Termite nest

Africa is home to more varieties of antelope than anywhere else in the world. Each species can be identified by its horns.

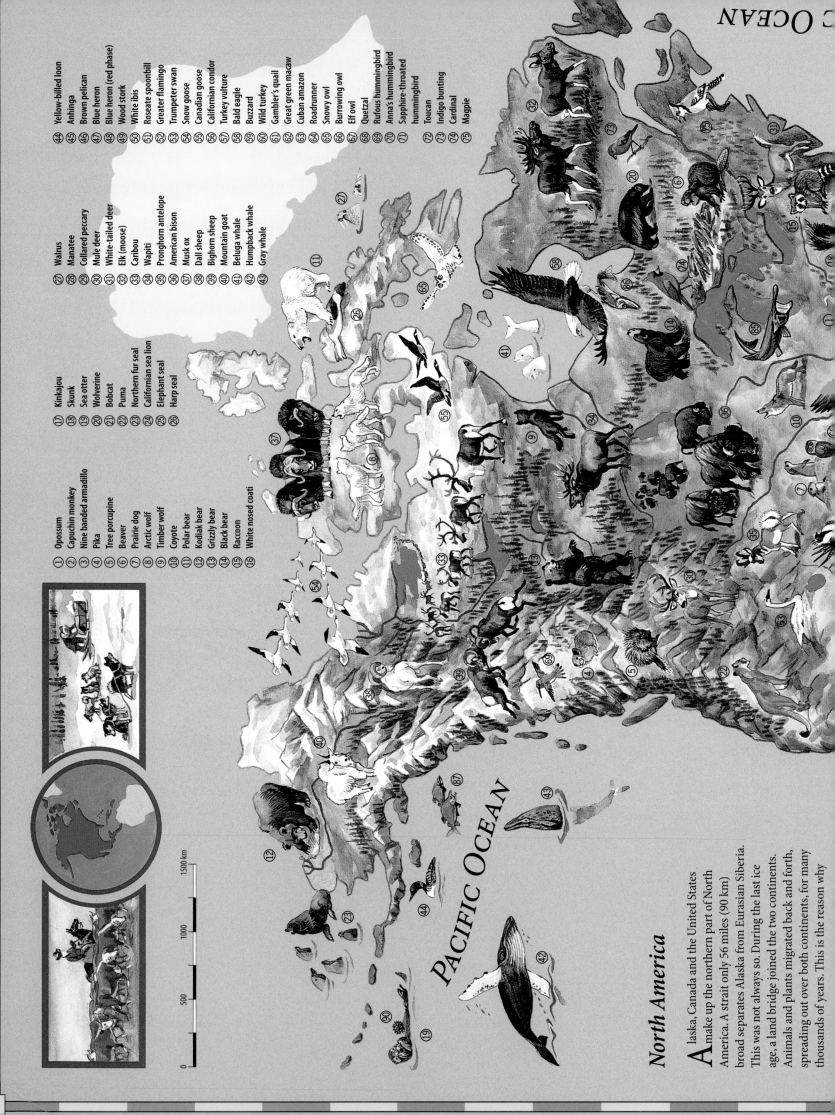

North America

Alaska, Canada and the United States make up the northern part of North America. A strait only 56 miles (90 km) broad separates Alaska from Eurasian Siberia. This was not always so. During the last ice age, a land bridge joined the two continents. Animals and plants migrated back and forth, spreading out over both continents, for many thousands of years. This is the reason why

PACIFIC OCEAN

1 Opossum
2 Capuchin monkey
3 Nine banded armadillo
4 Pika
5 Tree porcupine
6 Beaver
7 Prairie dog
8 Arctic wolf
9 Timber wolf
10 Coyote
11 Polar bear
12 Kodiak bear
13 Grizzly bear
14 Black bear
15 Raccoon
16 White nosed coati

17 Kinkajou
18 Skunk
19 Sea otter
20 Wolverine
21 Bobcat
22 Puma
23 Northern fur seal
24 Californian sea lion
25 Elephant seal
26 Harp seal

27 Walrus
28 Manatee
29 Collared peccary
30 Mule deer
31 White-tailed deer
32 Elk (moose)
33 Caribou
34 Wapiti
35 Pronghorn antelope
36 American bison
37 Musk ox
38 Dall sheep
39 Bighorn sheep
40 Mountain goat
41 Beluga whale
42 Humpback whale
43 Gray whale

44 Yellow-billed loon
45 Anhinga
46 Brown pelican
47 Blue heron
48 Blue heron (red phase)
49 Wood stork
50 White ibis
51 Roseate spoonbill
52 Greater flamingo
53 Trumpeter swan
54 Snow goose
55 Canadian goose
56 Californian condor
57 Turkey vulture
58 Bald eagle
59 Buzzard
60 Wild turkey
61 Gambler's quail
62 Great green macaw
63 Cuban amazon
64 Roadrunner
65 Snowy owl
66 Burrowing owl
67 Elf owl
68 Quetzal
69 Rufous hummingbird
70 Anna's hummingbird
71 Sapphire-throated hummingbird
72 Toucan
73 Indigo bunting
74 Cardinal
75 Magpie

0   500   1000   1500 km

there are so many similarities between some North American and Eurasian species.

For example, the caribou is the American cousin of the Eurasian reindeer, and the European red deer is very much like the American wapiti. European and Asian brown bears are related to the North American grizzly bear. There are, however, many other animal species found in the Americas that do not exist in Eurasia, including pronghorn antelope, skunk, armadillo and the tiny hummingbird.

North America remains a wide-open landscape, rich in animal life, particularly in the more thinly settled parts of Northern Canada and Alaska. The Rocky Mountains, extending from Mexico through the United States into Canada, have served as a north-south route for many different species, all the way down to the hot, dry desert. Cool, dark pine forests and rough mountain landscapes are the hunting grounds of the puma, also known as the mountain lion. The nearly extinct California condor, an enormous predatory bird with a wingspan of over 8 ft (3 m), also hunts there. The wide, grassy prairie is another typically North American environment. American bison are the habitat's largest land mammal, once travelling in enormous herds throughout the countryside. Bison were the means of survival for the Native American tribes. Smaller animals, like the prairie dog, a kind of ground squirrel, also thrive in the prairie. Many millions of these small creatures once lived in huge colonies, each inhabiting a seemingly endless network of underground chambers and tunnels. A secret tenant might be the burrowing owl, or a rattlesnake seeking shelter from the heat or cold. The coyote, a frequent character in Wild West stories or "Roadrunner" cartoons, is another resident of the prairie regions. It lives by hunting small animals, fish and carrion, but also by stealing domestic calves and lambs. For this reason, they are frequently tracked and killed by farmers. Further south, the pretty grassland gives way to dry, barren desert stretching deep into Mexico. The desert is home to the shy, but also very poisonous,

Gila monster and the speedy roadrunner. The latter survives by running down lizards and snakes. The elf owl, the world's smallest owl, lives in nest holes cut into the needled arms of the giant saguaro cactus.

The environment of most of eastern North America is wetter and greener. The entire landscape was once an enormous, endless forest before European settlers arrived to cut down the trees and put the plough to the land. A rich animal world still survives in the great lake and swamp areas. The magnificent bald eagle, with its powerful, raking talons, snatches fish out of the water in wetlands like the famous Florida Everglades. The Everglades, with its mild subtropical climate, is home to ibis, spoonbills, alligators and the

gentle manatee, also known as the sea cow.

Like a narrow bridge, Central America still joins the continents of North and South America as it has for the last 5 million years. Thousands of migratory birds make an annual journey through this land corridor, flying to and fro between their nesting places and winter quarters. The animals living in the Central American tropical rainforests are a mixture of northern and southern types. Capuchin and howler monkeys swing through the trees, while tapirs, jaguars and coatis make their way along the forest floor below. Spectacular toucans and parrots inhabit the hot lowlands. Colourful hummingbirds whirr through the air from flower to flower, their wings beating as many as 78 times per second. This allows them to virtually stand still in the air as they feed off a flower's sweet nectar.

- 76 Alligator snapping turtle
- 77 Alligator
- 78 Caiman
- 79 Rhino iguana
- 80 Basilisk
- 81 Gila monster
- 82 Boa

- 83 Rattlesnake
- 84 Copperhead
- 85 Paddlefish
- 86 Muskellunge
- 87 Pink salmon
- 88 Porcupine fish
- 89 Coral fish
- 90 Sea urchin

The wild mustangs of North America are descendants of European domestic breeds.

Europeans brought chaos and mindless slaughter to the great herds of bison. In 1900 there were very few remaining from the around 60 million American bison that once roamed the plains. On the very brink of extinction, a few herds were placed under protection.

This totem pole with its colourful animal carvings is evidence of the close bond of Native Americans with nature.

South America

South America was isolated from all other land masses for many millions of years.

For this reason, as was the case with Australia, there are animals here that died out a long time ago everywhere else, such as the marsupial opossum, the ancient three-toed sloth and the giant anteater. Once the Central American

land bridge came into being, animals from North America migrated in, such as the tapir and the jaguar, while animals that evolved in the tropics, like the opossum and armadillo,

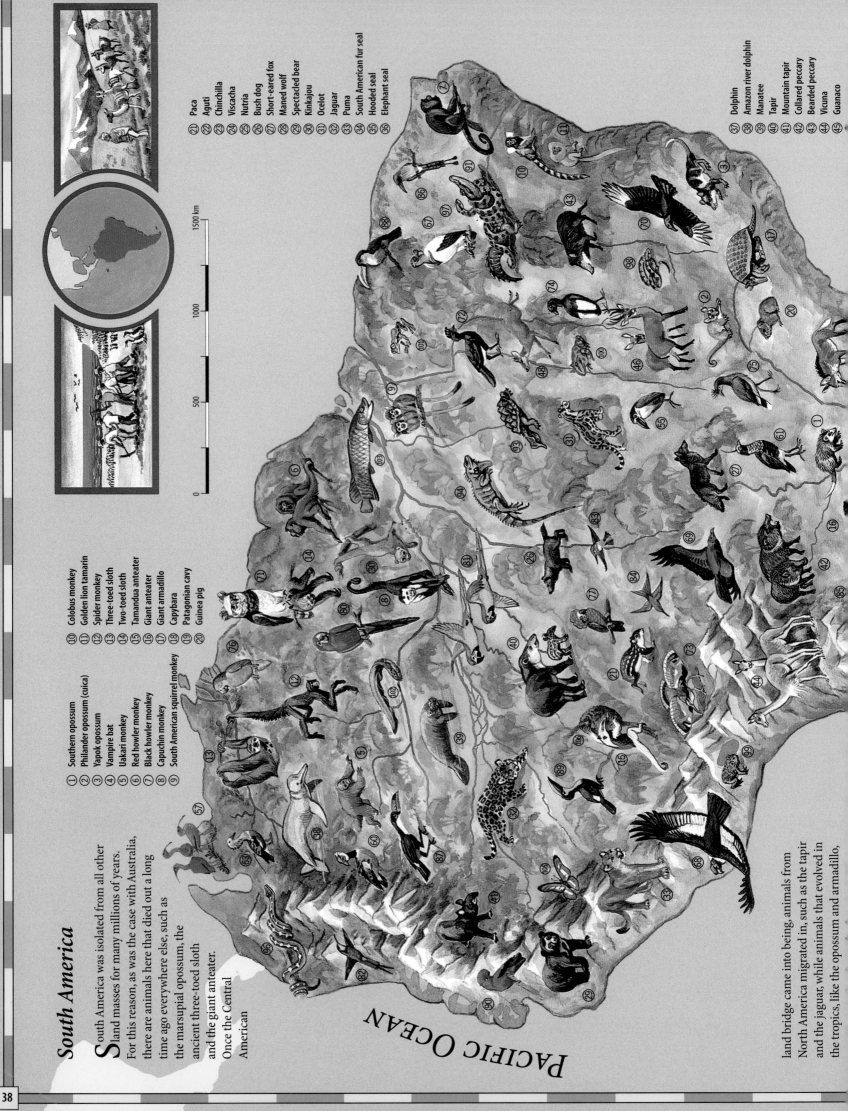

1 Southern opossum
2 Philander opossum (cuica)
3 Yapok opossum
4 Vampire bat
5 Uakari monkey
6 Red howler monkey
7 Black howler monkey
8 Capuchin monkey
9 South American squirrel monkey
10 Colobus monkey
11 Golden lion tamarin
12 Spider monkey
13 Three-toed sloth
14 Two-toed sloth
15 Tamandua anteater
16 Giant anteater
17 Giant armadillo
18 Capybara
19 Patagonian cavy
20 Guinea pig
21 Paca
22 Aguti
23 Chinchilla
24 Viscacha
25 Nutria
26 Bush dog
27 Short-eared fox
28 Maned wolf
29 Spectacled bear
30 Kinkajou
31 Ocelot
32 Jaguar
33 Puma
34 South American fur seal
35 Hooded seal
36 Elephant seal
37 Dolphin
38 Amazon river dolphin
39 Manatee
40 Tapir
41 Mountain tapir
42 Collared peccary
43 Bearded peccary
44 Vicuna
45 Guanaco

PACIFIC OCEAN

same is true of the guinea pig, which in South America is raised for food. The plains of the south are broad and treeless.

This is the home of the maned wolf, the giant, flightless rhea and the giant anteater. The latter uses its long, thin snout and sticky tongue to extract ants and termites from their nests. Interesting animals can be found even in the extreme dryness and heat of the Atacama Desert of Chile. Every year, thousands of flamingos flock to its salty lakes searching for food. The further south one travels, the stormier the climate becomes until one reaches the southern tip of the continent, Cape Horn, and the region known as Patagonia. The icy Antarctic is not far away,

The ovenbird builds an enclosed nest out of clay and grass.

ATLANTIC OCEAN

The Galapagos Islands are located in the Pacific Ocean off the north-west coast of the South American mainland. The islands are a unique animal habitat of giant land tortoises, marine iguana and the tiny Darwin finch. The islands are now a national park belonging to Ecuador.

and species like the elephant seal and South American fur seal are very much at home in the frigid coastlands. Only the green ocellated lizard survives this far south as a reminder of the tropical wonderland further north.

(3,000 m). This often cloud-covered landscape is called the Páramo.

Even here, rare species of hummingbird can be found sipping nectar. The most famous inhabitants of the Andes are the camelid species of guanacos and vicunas. These graze further south on the broad, grassy high plains. Llamas and alpacas were domesticated from wild guanaco stock by indigenous peoples many thousands of years ago. The

When threatened, the three-banded armadillo can roll itself up into an impregnable ball.

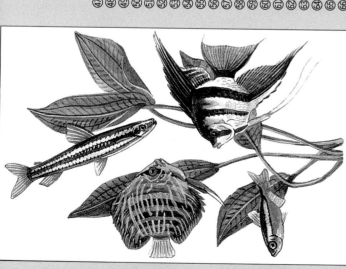

The Amazon River is home to innumerable species of colourful freshwater fish. Many Amazonian fish are popular aquarium pets.

northern half of South America is completely covered in dense rainforest, where the climate is oppressively hot and humid. The green forest canopy is inhabited not only by the hyacinth macaw, the largest parrot in the world, but also the harpy eagle, a large, predatory bird that can carry off a monkey. The fruits of the rainforest trees attract a large variety of monkeys, including the squirrel monkey, the red-furred ukari and the seldom seen golden lion tamarin. The tiny pygmy marmoset gnaws at tree bark, drinking the sap. Brightly coloured tree frogs are everywhere. Their bright red, green and yellow markings warn other animals of their poisonous skins. The famous poisoned arrows of the rain forest peoples are tipped with frog poison in preparation for the hunt. The cloudy rivers and streams of the primordial forest are home to river dolphins, anaconda snakes and piranhas.

The slopes of the Andes to the west are covered with more tranquil mountain forests at lower elevations. This is the home of the red Andean cock of the rock. The trees thin out and eventually disappear altogether at around 9,800 ft

47 Andes deer (huemul)
48 Mazama deer
49 Pudu
50 Rhea
51 Humboldt penguin
52 Galapagos penguin
53 Galapagos cormorant
54 Frigate bird
55 Boat-billed heron
56 Jabiru stork
57 Scarlet ibis
58 Andes flamingo
59 Chilean flamingo
60 Crested screamer
61 Horned screamer
62 Black necked swan
63 Orinoco goose
64 Andes goose
65 Magellan goose
66 Falkland steamerduck
67 King vulture

68 Condor
69 Turkey vulture
70 Black vulture
71 Harpy eagle
72 Hokko
73 Sun bittern
74 Grey-winged trumpeter
75 Seriema
76 Amazon parrot
77 Red fan parrot
78 Slender-billed parakeet
79 Austral conure
80 Hyacinth parrot
81 Macaw
82 Topaz hummingbird
83 Little woodstar
84 Swallow-tailed hummingbird
85 Red-tailed comet
86 Motmot
87 Giant toucan
88 Red-breasted toucan
89 Brown-backed toucan
90 Andes cock of the rock
91 Caiman
92 Galapagos giant tortoise

93 Matamata
94 Green iguana
95 Marine iguana
96 Dog-headed boa
97 Anaconda
98 Bushmaster
99 Titicaca frog
100 Horned toad
101 Monkey frog
102 Electric eel
103 Arapaima
104 Piranha
105 Blue morpho
106 Termite

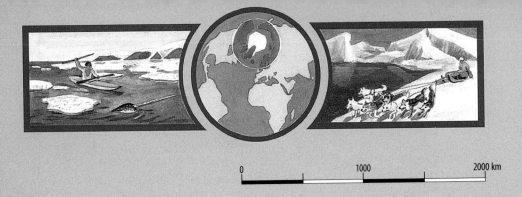

0   1000   2000 km

The Arctic

Many animals living inside the Arctic Circle in the far northern regions of Europe migrate south during the bitter cold days of winter, including the snow goose and whooper swan. Those that stay behind, like lemmings and seals, must rely on a thick coat or insulating layer of blubber to keep them warm.

1. Sperm whale
2. Orca (killer whale)
3. Narwhale
4. Beluga
5. Grey whale
6. Blue whale
7. Fin whale
8. Sei whale
9. Arctic wolf
10. Polar bear
11. Walrus
12. Hooded seal
13. Bearded seal
14. Ribbon seal
15. Polar ringed seal
16. Harp seal
17. Caribou
18. Reindeer
19. Musk ox
20. Snow goose
21. Whooper swan
22. Greenland shark
23. Cod

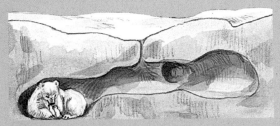

Polar bears are the largest predator of the arctic, but their cubs are born hairless, blind, deaf and barely larger than rats. Polar bears give birth in November or December in sheltered snow caves, which are warmed by body heat, just like igloos.

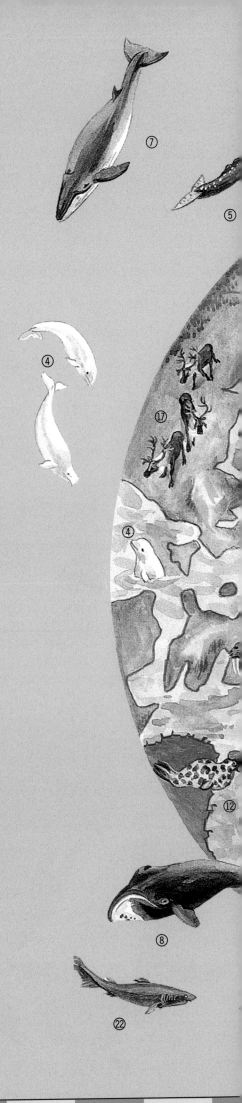

ARCTIC OCEAN

North Pole

ATLANTIC OCEAN

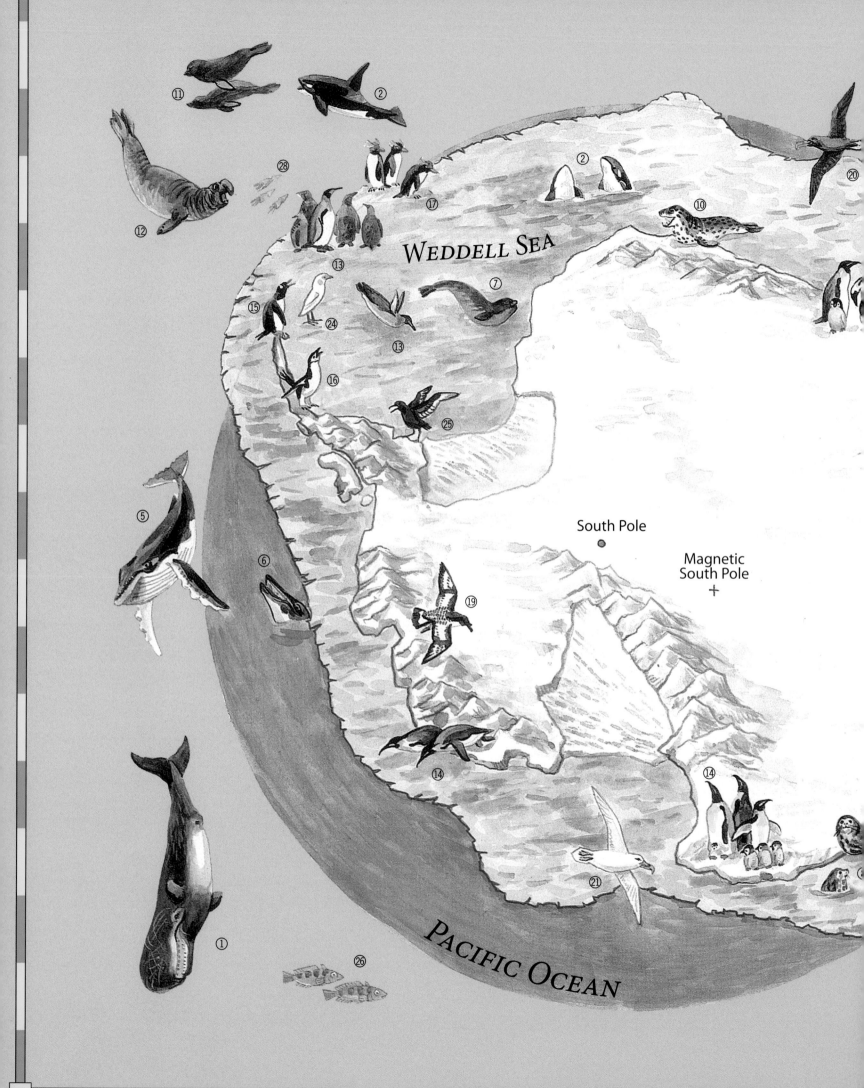

WEDDELL SEA

South Pole

Magnetic
South Pole
+

PACIFIC OCEAN

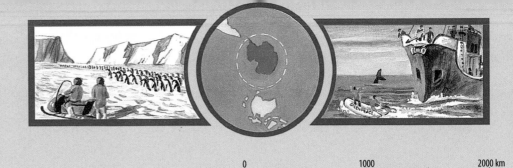

④

Antarctica

Krill, a tiny, reddish crustacean, is the most important food source in the icy south polar seas. It swarms in this part of the ocean in such great numbers that even the giant baleen whales can live off them. This is also the land of the penguins, always well dressed in their fine "tuxedos". On the ice they are waddling and inelegant, but once they dive into the sea they soar through the icy currents like arrows shot from a bow.

① Sperm whale
② Orca (killer whale)
③ Blue whale
④ Southern right whale
⑤ Humpback whale
⑥ Sei whale
⑦ Ross seal
⑧ Weddell seal
⑨ Crabeater seal
⑩ Leopard seal
⑪ Antarctic fur seal
⑫ Elephant seal
⑬ King penguin
⑭ Emperor penguin
⑮ Gentoo penguin
⑯ Chinstrap penguin
⑰ Rockhopper penguin
⑱ Adelie penguin
⑲ Cape petrel
⑳ Northern giant petrel
㉑ Southern giant petrel
㉒ Snow petrel
㉓ Antarctic cormorant
㉔ Snowy sheathbill
㉕ Skua
㉖ Antarctic cod
㉗ Mackerel icefish
㉘ Squid